Community
and
Commitment

Community and Commitment

John Driver

Introduction by
Wilbert Shenk

HERALD PRESS
Scottdale, Pennsylvania
Kitchener, Ontario

COMMUNITY AND COMMITMENT
Copyright © 1976 by Herald Press, Scottdale, Pa. 15683
    Published simultaneously in Canada by Herald Press,
    Kitchener, Ont. N2G 4M5
Library of Congress Catalog Card Number: 76-41463
International Standard Book Number: 0-8361-1802-2
Printed in the United States of America
Design: Alice B. Shetler

10 9 8 7 6 5 4 3 2

To brothers and sisters on three continents who are concerned to discover more faithful ways of being God's people in the world.

CONTENTS

Introduction by Wilbert R. Shenk 9

Author's Preface 13

1. Discerning God's Will Afresh 15

2. A Community of Sharing..................... 28

3. A Community of Forgiveness 41

4. A Community of Gifts 54

5. A Community of Peace 68

6. A Missionary Community 80

The Author............................... 93

INTRODUCTION

The challenge of church renewal is to avoid the palliative approach. Cheap renewal, like cheap grace, falsifies the gospel.

One temptation is to seek renewal so that the church might become successful. Success is self-validating in Western society. A program or industry is measured by its growth rate; growth equals success. The church which can report annual increases in membership and an expanding church plant is successful.

Another pitfall is to concentrate on relevance. The church should not become a museum piece. The gospel should be believable and presented in a winning manner. Rather than the church presuming to know what the world needs, the world should set the agenda for action for the church. The measure of the church's relevance is its degree of success.

Biblical prophecy is attuned to another key. God's prophets in the Old Testament recalled His people to authenticity and faithfulness. Jesus, the greatest of the prophets, true to His nature and calling, accepted the way of the cross. By every worldly standard His life was unsuccessful. The gospel of Jesus Christ has been and always will be "a stone of stumbling and a rock of offense." The hallmark of genuine renewal will be the degree to which it calls the church to rediscover and experience its authenticity. In so doing, the church will be equipped to serve faithfully.

Those concerned for the quality and vitality of the church's life today are asking fundamental questions. What exactly is the nature of the church? What is the purpose of the church in God's plan? What are the marks of healthy church life? What is the relationship between the church's inner life and its witness to the world?

At particular moments in history important new currents began to flow which carried the church in new directions. Sometimes these have been good, at other times detrimental. When the emperor Constantine made Christianity the state religion in AD 313, a course was set which changed the character of Christianity for centuries. Springing from widespread longing for a fresh word from heaven, the sixteenth-century Reformation movement tried to reverse the excesses and abuses of the past.

By the eighteenth century, church life had sunk again to a low ebb and the masses were in great spiritual poverty. George Whitefield and the Wesleys set the pace for a revival movement based on an unvarnished message of repentance and conversion. Whitefield was the greater preacher, but John Wesley was the superior leader. He recognized that new believers needed fellowship, nurture, and discipline, and proceeded to organize cell groups. Beginning in the nineteenth century the modern missionary movement was launched, a movement which has completely altered the world Christian map.

Every movement to renew the church is, by definition, dedicated to producing new seriousness in church life and a degree of authenticity which has been lacking. Both the form and dynamic of the church's life is important. To discern God's will for His people will require more than listening to the world's drumbeat. God's call to His people today will be heard clearly only by a reverent and intense listening to His Word under the illumination of His Spirit. John Driver is a sure and sensitive guide for us in this process.

Wilbert R. Shenk
Overseas Secretary
Mennonite Board of Missions

AUTHOR'S PREFACE

Community and Commitment grows out of efforts within the church on three continents to discern God's will for His people and to discover the shape that obedience to His will takes in our world. To acknowledge my indebtedness to this brotherhood of international dimensions is only right.

Many of the ideas elaborated in these chapters have already been developed more eloquently by teachers within the North American brotherhood. Representatives of this group are H. S. Bender, John H. Yoder, John W. Miller, and C. Norman Kraus. The many references to their works will be obvious to the reader acquainted with their writings.

Most of the facets of the vision of the church set forth in these pages have been discussed and tested by members of the Montevideo seminary community, as well as by other congregations of discerning disciples in Uruguay and Argentina.

These concerns have also been shared in Spain with Plymouth Brethren and Baptist congregations where similar concerns were echoed by a number of brothers and sisters sensitive to the needs and mission of the church in that land.

Excepting chapter five, the material was first presented in essentially its present form at the forty-third annual conference of the Argentine Mennonite Church in January 1974. These studies were published later in the year in Spanish by Ediciones Certeza in Buenos Aires as *Comunidad y Compromiso: Estudios Sobre la Renovación de la Iglesia.* The content of chapter five was first shared with the congregation which meets together at 191 Verdi Street in Barcelona, Spain.

These experiences illustrate the transcultural nature of the good news of God's saving purpose in Jesus Christ. The apostolic witness to the reality of the messianic community and to the forms which its life took in their world still speaks in our day. It instructs people everywhere who are concerned to discern God's will. It guides those who, in true repentance, are willing to shape their common life in the Spirit in accordance with God's intention for the human family as it has been made known most fully in the person of His Messiah and that community which bears His name.

John Driver
August 1976

1. DISCERNING GOD'S WILL AFRESH

Renewal which really renews

Many serious Christians today are concerned about renewal in the church. Pleas for renewal are not new. In fact, renewal has been a continuing concern among the people of God throughout history. Generation after generation of Hebrew prophets arose to call God's people to return to the paths of faithfulness. New Testament apostles warned the messianic communities against deformations which had already begun to appear in the church during the first generation.

In the nineteen centuries which have followed, concern for renewal in the Christian church, sometimes strong and other times weak, has never been absent. At times these voices spoke from within the institutional church. On other occasions prophetic persons and movements arose on the fringes of the official church, calling for revitalization of the body of Christ.

So the presence of voices calling the church to renewal in our time should not surprise or threaten us. Pleas for renewal should instead be welcome as a sign of life and potential growth. The church will do well to listen carefully, for its continuing life depends upon its willingness to repent and be renewed. There is no other alternative. Either we will be renewed in sincere repentance, or we will cease to be the church of Jesus Christ.

Authentic renewal in the church arises out of intense desire to know the will of God in order to experience deeper dimensions of obedience. As the people of God we receive joyfully all calls for renewal which are rooted in a desire to know and serve our Lord.

Both church history and personal experience teach us that renewal is a relative term. Like revolution and other popular terms, renewal risks losing its real meaning with use. Revolution, for example, has come to mean "that which comes to occupy the place of its predecessor." The term is applied equally to new rightist military governments and to products which some advertising agency wants to sell. So we have revolutionary army generals whose political program is anything but new, and revolutionary deodorants which merely appear in a different package with a new name. Some attempts at church renewal are similarly superficial. Not all changes introduced into the church in the name of renewal are authentic. Not all grow out of a desire to know God's will and experience greater obedience.

How, then, do we experience authentic renewal? Authentic renewal is no easy thing. It implies change and change is often painful. The change which renewal brings affects our present situation, as well as our future. In testing renewal experiences we need to look closely at how the past is viewed. It cannot be viewed in isolation from the experience of God's people rooted in the past.

Movements of renewal frequently take a negative attitude toward history. They attempt to forget the past and begin afresh—a new beginning from zero. Some voices suggest that all that is necessary is to go back to reading the Bible and somehow we'll find ourselves on the right track again. But it isn't that simple. Although we might like to begin from zero, our mentality and orientation have been formed by our experience. We are conditioned by our own often unfaithful past. God's people cannot hope for radical renewal without some reference to their roots. Historical perspective furnishes a point of reference for renewal, enabling us to see ourselves as we really are.

Jesus Christ is normative

Like all movements in the history of God's people which have led to authentic renewal, today's attempts must center renewal around a normative reference point. Sixteenth-century Anabaptists found normativeness in the New Testament church. Their sources concerning the first-century community were the New Testament documents. Their norm was not the primitive church as it actually was, however, but rather the apostolic vision of what the life of the church should be in Christ. They did not want merely to imitate the church of the New Testament period, but rather to take seriously the authority of the apostles as interpreters and teachers of Jesus. This does not imply that the New Testament period was a golden age whose forms were to be imitated. One does not have to read far in the epistles to discover the fallible nature of the apostolic church. Thus the Anabaptists sought renewal not in mere imitation of an earlier church, but in seeking the normative reference point around which the church was centered.

For the apostolic church and for the church of all ages that reference point is Jesus Christ. We confess that Jesus Christ is Lord. According to this confession Jesus Christ is Lord of the present (although what one observes in the life of many congregations may lead us to question this). And certainly Jesus Christ will also be Lord of the future.

What forms will the lordship of Christ take? This question is important because its answer has implications for the forms which church renewal should take.

The Christ who is our normative reference point in determining the shape of the renewed future in which His lordship will be manifest with greater clarity can only be known to us through the incarnation of the past. In the incarnation God has most clearly revealed His nature (Hebrews 1:1-3). Jesus Christ has initiated the church in its mission. Therefore the life and mission of the church must always remain under the judgment of Jesus, or of the New Testament in which we find authoritative witness to Him. It is not a matter of finding in the New Testament recipes for the needs of the church in every conceivable situation. Rather, the New Testament is our only authoritative testimony to Jesus, our norm.

The shape which the incarnation took in Jesus, and His impact on life in the apostolic community, demonstrate the shape of authentic renewal in both present and future. With Christ as Lord we follow in His footsteps of suffering obedience and servanthood.

So, in its attempts to renew its life, the church must continually return to the incarnation, to Jesus and the apostolic witness to Him. Jesus gives meaning and authority to what the church does, thereby bringing it under the judgment of God. This is not a matter of making a new start from zero. It is a way of moving ahead in history with Jesus Christ as the determinative norm for the life of the church. It is an attempt to leap over the unfaithfulness and the deformations of the recent past to the incarnation in order to reorient and reform the direction of the church. To the degree that this process requires a return to the roots of the church in the person of Jesus Christ it may be called authentic, or radical, reformation.

Radical renewal in the history of God's people

Radical renewal is no novelty. Numerous examples occur in the experience of the people of God; for example, Solomon's prayer recorded in 2 Chronicles 7:14: "If my people who are called by my name humble themselves, and pray and seek my face, and turn from their wicked ways, then I will hear from heaven, and will forgive their sin and heal their land." Authentic renewal implied conversion (turn or return) from disobedience to Israel's normative and constitutive event, which, as we learn from the context, was the Exodus (2 Chronicles 6:5).

The Old Testament prophets leaped over the period of the monarchy in which they lived back to Moses and the Exodus in order to pronounce judgment on Israel's current infidelity. They pointed out the foundation of Israel's vocation at Sinai and invited them to authentic renewal as God's people (for example, Hosea 11:1-4; 12:9, 10; Jeremiah 2:2, 3; Isaiah 40:3).

Jesus used a similar approach when the Pharisees attempted to trap Him with a question on divorce. Because of the hardness of men's hearts, Moses had permitted divorce under certain circumstances. But Jesus passed over these moral concessions of the Mosaic era with an appeal to the will of God Himself as revealed in the creation of man and woman. Ethical concessions made in the ongoing history of God's people are judged in the light of a normative authority—God's original intention (Mark 10:1-9). Jesus also used this method in the Sermon on the Mount to show that the function of law is to point toward the fulfillment of God's original intention for human social relationships.

In his attempt to establish the priority of faith over works of law as God's way to justify man, Paul appealed back past Moses to Abraham (Galatians 3). Later Montanus and Tertullian, in the face of growing institutionalization of authority in the church, appealed back to Pentecost. Such historical examples can be multiplied: Francis of Assisi, Peter Waldo and the Poor Men of Lyons, Peter Chelcicky and the Czech Brethren, the Anabaptists, George Fox and the Friends of Truth. All of these were attempts to renew the church by leaping back over the teachings and practice of the church of their time and appealing to the roots of the life of God's people found in the scriptural witness.

Renewal or reformation means making ethical decisions in accord with the Spirit of Jesus as He is known in the incarnation through the apostolic witness. Unless the church orients its attempts at renewal toward that incarnation it will run the risk of straying off course.

In face of our need for renewal we are sometimes tempted to see only two alternatives: either we seek to renew our life in light of the desperate situation in which we find ourselves, or we simply resign ourselves to the apparent necessity of continuing as we are. Renewal which looks only at the actual situation in which the church finds itself is destined to be superficial. Instead, we must return to the church's normative roots willing to pay the high price of repentance and obedience, the only path to real renewal and radical reformation.

Reading and interpreting the Bible

If the form church renewal takes is to be determined by the Spirit, and words and deeds of Jesus, then it is essential to take the New Testament seriously. We must not only read the Bible, but must read it in an appropriate manner. All Christians share concern for reading the Scriptures. Yet Christians differ considerably in approaches and interpretation.

In the course of the sixteenth-century reformation four approaches to biblical interpretation were articulated and tested by various groups of Christians concerned with renewal. As historians remind us, there are a number of similarities between the period of rapid social change which characterized the sixteenth century and our own times. And this is certainly true of approaches to the interpretation of Scripture.

1. *Rule of faith:* The Bible is simply interpreted in the same general way in which the church has been accustomed to interpreting it. The traditional faith and practice of the church largely determine the stance from which the Bible is read. This approach has been common among Protestants as well as Catholics. Believers and congregations who read in this way are "confirmed" in their "faith." But such faith will probably be a traditional faith which, depending on the situation, may be more or less consonant with the Spirit, and words and deeds of Jesus.

In the sixteenth century this hermeneutic principle was called the *rule of faith.* The church tends to be confirmed in its faith, but this kind of hermeneutic slams the door on any possibility of renewal. The Bible read and interpreted in this way keeps things as they are.

2. *Rule of love:* Another way in which Christians have often used the Bible has been to limit the interpretations to those which seemed to be possible or feasible. In the debates carried on during the sixteenth century this hermeneutical option was called the *rule of love.* That is, love or patience for the weaker member in the church led Christians to soften interpretations which led to hard moral decisions in order to ease the situation of those who did not find costly discipleship to Jesus within their range of possibilities.

This is the hermeneutical principle which has often been applied to Jesus' teachings regarding love for enemies and the prohibition of vengeance (Matthew 5:38-48); His prohibition of the oath (Matthew 5:33-37); His command to share goods with those in need without charging interest (Matthew 6:19-21; Luke 6:34); His word to His disciples forbidding the exercise of coercive power (Mark 10:41-45).

Some in the church were willing and able to take seriously this ethic, but to interpret these teachings as applicable to all of the church constituted a lack of love for the weaker. This principle of biblical interpretation has not been limited to the sixteenth century, but has found wide acceptance in the church. Many times it is practiced quite unconsciously, but the problem is no less real.

The matter of reading the Bible and interpreting it properly is not merely a question of biblicism, as it is often understood, but rather one which has to do with our concept of discipleship and radical obedience. It has to do with the fundamental nature of the church. Even though the Bible is read, things don't change much in the church as a result of this approach.

3. *Rule of Paul:* Another way of reading and interpreting the Bible finds its inspiration in Paul's writings, "Let two or three prophets speak, and let the others weigh what is said" (1 Corinthians 14:29). Accordingly, this hermeneutical principle has traditionally been called the *rule of Paul.* The context indicates that this process was to be carried out in the assemblies of the Christian community.

The function of prophets was to expound the will of God as it had been revealed to them in the Scriptures, although the immediate form of the revelation might be indirect as well as direct. The function of the rest of the congregation was to hear the message of the prophets, and then weigh or discern the message over against the other criteria for discernment which was at their disposal—their own common experience as disciples of Jesus; other voices in the community, apostles, teachers, other prophets, presiders.

What is basic, as well as novel (and this is true of the twentieth century as well as the sixteenth) in this concept, is that the congregation is recognized as the place where the will of God can best be interpreted. The gathered congregation, rather than its authorities, theologians, and prophets, is responsible for discerning the will of God. In the exercise of his hermeneutic prerogative the common ordinary Christian acts as a full member of the body of Christ.

Wherever Christians assemble in a common search for solution to the problems of disobedience, there the Holy Spirit makes clear the meaning of the Scriptures. The full participation of the congregation in the hermeneutic process does not make unnecessary the functions of prophet and teacher in the church. Their revealing and clarifying roles should be recognized. But their special activity is limited to the exercise of their particular gifts. In this process the importance of one who presides is obvious because the moderating function is fundamental in all congregational process.

This form of interpreting the Bible does not negate the historical tradition of the church, but simply refuses to grant to tradition an authoritative role. This vision limits the authority of traditional creeds, or special confessions of faith, as well as that of constituted ecclesiastical authorities. It rather gives the gathered congregation the right as well as the obligation to read and interpret the Scriptures.

4. *Rule of Christ:* Another New Testament passage which underlines the fundamental importance of a common hermeneutical process is the one known traditionally as the *rule of Christ* (Matthew 18:15-20). The presence of the Spirit of Christ is promised when the congregation assembles to discern the will of God so that it can make ethical decisions in obedience to Christ (Matthew 16:19; 18:15-20; John 20:22, 23). The *rule of Christ* adds two important dimensions to our understanding of the way the church is to read and interpret the Bible.

a. Disposed to obedience—It is especially noteworthy that the authority to make ethical decisions of a binding character in the church came after Peter's confession that Jesus is the Christ, the Messiah. Only that community which confesses Jesus as Lord is divinely authorized to interpret the will of God and to make ethical decisions consonant to it. Only that community of disciples which seeks

to know and obey the will of God can read and interpret
the Scripture with integrity.

Jesus said, "If any man's will is to do his [God's] will, he
shall know whether the teaching is from God" (John
7:17). This fact became clear in the experience of Jesus'
disciples. "And by this we may be sure that we know him,
if we keep his commandments" (1 John 2:3).

This fact is important for understanding the nature of
religious knowledge as well as the way we must operate to
read and interpret the Scriptures rightly. Sound interpretation apparently does not depend so much on the
clarity of the exegetical work of theologians (although
their role in clarifying the biblical texts and reconstruc-
ting the historical contexts are certainly important) as on
the disposition to obedience of the community of disciples
in which the Bible is read and interpreted.

b. Committed to discernment—The *rule of Christ*
teaches us that God's Word is to be interpreted to discern
His will and find solutions to the problems of specific disobedience within the community. The will of God will be
known in the process of binding and loosing in concrete
cases of questionable conduct within the church so that
persons may be reconciled in obedience to Jesus.

The writers of the New Testament record on only two
occasions Jesus using the term "church" (Matthew 16:18;
18:17). But the fact that both times he used the term in
relation to this congregational process of discernment
serves to underscore its importance. Reading and interpreting the Bible is not of secondary importance in the life
of the Christian community, but basic to its very existence. The church exists fundamentally where brothers
and sisters read and interpret together God's Word in

order to discover concrete ways of truly being disciples
of Jesus, and in the process are reconciled with one
another in Christ.

Discerning God's will afresh

In conclusion, these four keys of biblical interpretation
were tested during the Reformation of the sixteenth
century—rule of faith, rule of love, rule of Paul, and rule
of Christ. Of these options, only the last two led to the
openness which made possible a close look at the New
Testament to discern what faithfulness to Christ might
mean at that time. In church renewal Bible reading and interpretation play a fundamental role.

But if renewal is to be authentic and really radical, then
openness before God and our brothers and sisters and
willingness to repent and to submit to the lordship of
Christ in costly obedience are required. "Not every one
who says to me, 'Lord, Lord,' shall enter the kingdom of
heaven, but he who does the will of my Father who is in
heaven" (Matthew 7:21).

These Bible studies are offered in response to the desire
for renewal in our midst. May we discern afresh the will of
God in our lives and grow together as a community of disciples truly committed to Jesus.

1. We cannot but lament that spirit of self-
centeredness and individualism so characteristic of
modern Western society, and which prevails even in the
midst of the community which confesses the name of
Jesus Christ. What does the New Testament say about the
concrete forms which that communion which God offers
us through His Spirit will take in the body of Christ?

2. We are concerned at the apparent lack in our midst

of the commitment and ethical seriousness which characterized discipleship in the New Testament community. Moved by the Spirit of Jesus, how can we help one another live up to our best intentions as disciples of Christ?

3. There is a sincere concern in our midst to discover and experience the authentic expressions of the power of God's Spirit in the church. How can we receive and exercise in obedience all the gifts that the Spirit of Christ bestows upon His body so that we may be more fully that community in which His Spirit dwells and acts?

4. We are appalled by that unbiblical polarization between the "spiritual" and the "social" aspects of the church's life and mission which has come to characterize much of modern Western Christian thought. Is it not possible for the community which confesses Jesus Christ as Lord to demonstrate with integrity the wholeness of the gospel of peace which has come through Jesus Christ?

5. In light of the evangelizing mission which Jesus entrusted to His community, we ask ourselves with all seriousness, what is really the essence of the good news which we are to live and proclaim? And what does it mean to make disciples of Jesus Christ in our time?

2. THE CHURCH:
A COMMUNITY OF SHARING

To be or not to be a community is not an option for the church. By nature the church is a community and experiences communion. But the question before the people of God is: What kind of community will we be?

Definitions

In the New Testament the most expressive term used to describe the common life lived in the body of Christ is *koinonia*. In its various forms and derivatives, koinonia appears some fifty times in the Greek New Testament and means "that which is held in common." It is translated variously as: fellowship, common, contribution, share, participation, partners, partake, partnership, generous. So the term carries a wide range of meaning. It is used about equally in the New Testament to express spiritual sharing, and sharing in a concrete, material way. Thus the meaning of "fellowship" or "communion" in the New Testament relates to sharing one common life within the body of Christ at all the levels of existence and experience—spiritual, social, intellectual, economic. No area of life can be excluded.

Koinonia means having a part in something in which others also have a part, conscious sharing of something we hold in common, a life consciously grounded in a common element—Jesus Christ and His Spirit. True Christian community or fellowship is created and sustained in a common faith, a common life in Christ, a common commitment of obedience to Christ as Lord. In short, it is participating together in life in His Spirit. The strength and quality of Christian fellowship depends directly on the intensity and integrity of these foundational relationships.

This brief review of the meaning of koinonia in the New Testament suggests how impoverished have been the traditional concepts of community or fellowship or communion held by the church. Koinonia is more than meeting together from time to time; it is more than merely enjoying the presence of others; it is more than those feelings of well-being which warm our hearts when we greet our friends at church functions; it is more than common ethnic, cultural, linguistic, and historical ties (although these may well represent important psychological and sociological values); it is more than the organization of a congregation into a series of subgroups related to interest, age, and sex (such multiplication of activities can become a substitute for true koinonia).

So the meaning of Christian community or fellowship is much deeper than the terms community or fellowship in their sociological dimensions. In this study we seek to discover that "moreness" which characterizes the authentic koinonia of the church of Jesus Christ.

Koinonia in Jerusalem

In his description of the new people of God immediately after Pentecost, Luke mentions four characteristics of life in the church: "And they devoted themselves to [1] the apostles' teaching and [2] fellowship, to [3] the breaking

of bread and [4] the prayers" (Acts 2:42). Those who had
called upon the Lord in repentance and faith and who had
received the Holy Spirit found themselves irresistibly
drawn to one another within the body of Christ. The
manner in which they shared the marvelous works of God
in their midst was so intense and so continuous that their
relationship is described as koinonia, which can be
translated as fellowship, community of life, or communion (common union) with one another.

In this experience they were distinguished from the rest
of the Jews, for the Spirit of God was uniquely at work in
their midst creating koinonia. They felt their new unity in-
tensely. Their experience of spiritual communion had an
immediate effect upon their social relationship, producing a new community with social and economic dimensions. They took time together sharing food in one
another's houses with great joy and transparent sincerity.
They were described as being of "one heart and soul" and
this led them to share their possessions so that "there was
not a needy person among them" because "no one said
that any of the things which he possessed was his own, but
they had everything in common" (Acts 4:32-34).

In this process individual particularity was superseded
in all its aspects—heart, soul, and possessions—so that a
person was free to participate fully with others in the new
community of Jesus. Community for these people included full sharing of all dimensions of human well-being,
even the concrete elements of daily sustenance. But these
men and women did not set out simply to establish a new
economic order. The Spirit of God empowered their lives
in such a way that even their economic practices were
reordered.

The teaching of the apostles was a common possession shared by all. The message of Christ was a common possession shared by all. The spiritual riches of grace and the power of God manifested in Christ and through the Holy Spirit were common possessions shared by all.

Likewise, material possessions became common possessions to be shared among all. This is simply a matter of Christian love, of the love of God made operative in the new community of Pentecost. One can readily understand why common meals celebrated within the brotherhood came to be known as *agape,* for that is the point at which the expression of love became concrete within the brotherhood. The church is a community of love in action. Authentic Christian love exists only in action (see Romans 13:8, 10).

The concrete forms which koinonia took in the life of the Christian community in Jerusalem should not be seen as an impractical exception. Economic sharing in the Jerusalem community is sometimes cited as a cause of the subsequent economic need of the church to which Gentile churches responded with their gifts. While this interpretation seems natural in a capitalistically oriented approach, we must recognize our limitations in assigning causes to the later economic crisis in the Jerusalem brotherhood. In our understanding of the Jerusalem experience we dare not overlook its precedent in the life of Jesus and His disciples. That same spirit of sharing continues to orient the life of the church afterward (for example, Romans 12:13).

Koinonia in Corinth

Another passage basic to our understanding of koinonia in the New Testament church is I Corinthians 10

and 11, where Paul attempts to correct the deformations
which had come to characterize the celebration of the
Lord's Supper in Corinth. If we could free ourselves of the
filter of centuries of ecclesiastical practices and eucharistic debates, we might see in the words "the cup" and
"the bread" a reference to the daily practice of Jesus and
His disciples, that of sharing a common meal.

The Last Supper of Jesus with His disciples was eaten
as part of celebrating the Jewish Passover. Although a
special occasion, it was at the same time another in a long
series of common meals which Jesus and His disciples had
been eating together since they left their occupations to
follow Jesus and to share the life, the purse, and the table
of their Lord.

Following the crucifixion the disciples continued the
practice of eating together. Precisely on these occasions
the risen Lord most frequently appeared—in the upper
room in Jerusalem, in the inn at Emmaus, by the seaside
in Galilee.

That the community of the disciples should continue
the intimate communion of a common meal after Pentecost seems only natural. The practice was not merely
religious or spiritual, but also carried social and economic
dimensions. To share possessions in a simple society is to
share food, because one's daily bread is about all the
wealth to which a common man can aspire. So in a real
sense the Christian church could be defined, at least in
part, as that community where members share their bread
and wine.

Later this simple form of sharing possessions, as well as
other aspects of life in the community of the Messiah, was
propagated through the missionary vitality of the

primitive church beyond the confines of Judaism to the Gentile world. But here Christians were confronted by a new and dangerous situation as they brought their forms of community with them into non-Jewish society. They found that the Gentiles also celebrated their religious banquets, but for different reasons.

So we find the new Gentile Christians in Corinth bringing their old customs, and in the process deforming the practice as well as denying the principles underlying the communion of the Lord's table. According to custom it was possible for "each one to go ahead with his own meal" (1 Corinthians 11:21) forgetting that this constituted a denial of koinonia. It was this pagan deformation which Paul sought to correct with his warning to "any one who eats and drinks without discerning the body" (11:29). In light of the very nature of life within the body of Christ it is a contradiction for "each one" to pretend to do his own thing.

Communion presupposes a community which shares its life. The symbols of this commonality lack meaning outside of the reality of the community of Jesus Christ where life is shared in the power of His Spirit. The eucharistic tradition of Protestants and Catholics alike has tended to hide from view the concrete reality of koinonia. Concern for sacramental channels of grace on one hand and the safeguarding of a doctrinally adequate view of symbolism on the other have both blinded the church to the fundamental importance of commonality in the body of Christ.

The New Testament invites us to formulate a theology and practice of communion according to the true nature of the body of Christ, freeing us from the temptation to

separate the symbol from the reality which we seek to
symbolize. Eating and drinking at the Lord's table is but
one concrete element in all that authentic koinonia means
in the community of Jesus.

Jesus and koinonia

Jesus had many things to say to His followers concerning their life together in the new community of the
Messiah. The Sermon on the Mount is packed with instructions to guide the common life of His disciples; for
example, interpersonal relationships which are free from
judgmental attitudes, anger, and hatred. But above all, we
find instructive His teachings concerning possessions. A
fundamental parallelism in the Sermon is often not noticed: Jesus' attitude toward coercion and violence
(Matthew 5:38-48) and His attitude toward possessions
(6:19-34). The same parallelism is found in Paul's treat-
ment of these matters. He sets the two themes in jux-
taposition in Romans 12:13, 14.

While Mennonites have tended to heed with
seriousness Jesus' teachings on coercive power and
violence, they have been less sensitive to His teachings
concerning material possessions. Should we not take with
equal seriousness both segments of instruction? Both bear
the stamp of Jesus' authority. In both cases, survival
depends on God's providential care.

The practice of Jesus' economic ethic, as well as His
teaching on nonresistance, places the disciple in a
vulnerable position in relation to society. Sharing
possessions along with renouncing the right to exercise
coercion are both utter leaps of faith in the kind of society
in which we live. Of course we do well to remember that

Jesus' teachings should be understood in the context of a messianic community. We have often confused the issues and then written Jesus' ethic off as impractical because of the modern individualistic mentality which has characterized our approach to these texts.

Jesus' first commandment concerning the use of possessions is this: "Do not lay up for yourselves treasures on earth . . . but lay up for yourselves treasures in heaven." This is done by being generous toward others (Luke 12:21, 32-34; 18:22). In this way Jesus invites His disciples to become a community characterized by its generosity—a community in which those who possess take the initiative and share with those who need. In this way Jesus seeks to free His disciples from the tyranny of possessions so that they may serve others in love.

A second commandment of Jesus concerning possessions warns His followers against anxiety. "Do not be anxious about your life . . . what you shall eat . . . what you shall drink . . . what you shall put on" (Matthew 6:25, 31, 34). When we are honest enough to admit it, we will recognize that a major portion of our anxieties and concerns have to do with precisely those things which guarantee our survival. But Jesus warns that this is really a pagan attitude. He calls us to live not as pagans but as the people of God. The remedy which He offers is trusting ourselves to the provident care of our heavenly Father within the context of the new community of the Messiah.

Jesus' third commandment is a résumé of His scale of priorities: "But seek first his kingdom and his righteousness, and all these things shall be yours as well" (Matthew 6:33). This attitude toward possessions is radically revolutionary. Human beings tend to think of themselves and their own needs before others. But Jesus calls for turning this around. He invites His followers to seek that community of love which anticipates the kingdom of God, in which life, including possessions, is shared. He promises that all needs will be provided.

How this promise will be fulfilled is discovered in another passage: "Truly, I say to you, there is no one who has left house or brothers or sisters or mother or father or children or lands, for my sake and for the gospel, who will not receive a hundredfold now in this time, houses and brothers and sisters and mothers and children and lands, with persecutions, and in the age to come eternal life" (Mark 10:29, 30). To those who leave all to follow Jesus He promises a new community in which life is shared. He invites His disciples to form a community where a family spirit dominates, where no one lives for himself alone, where a person, even though he must leave what is his, will find family and home and all that he needs among the believing community. The needs of Jesus' followers, even though they be persecuted, will be provided by a loving Father who works through the generous community of His people.

The expressions of koinonia which characterized the church in Jerusalem were simply an extension of life in the community of disciples gathered around Jesus, practiced through the power of the Spirit of God poured out upon His people.

Koinonia and brotherhood

Another way of expressing koinonia in the New Testament is the use of "brethren" to designate the church as well as individual members of Christ's body. The term most frequently used in the New Testament to designate Christians, brethren, is used some 250 times in Acts and the epistles. Its use is so frequent because it is the most natural greeting in such a community. It is a brotherhood which is born out of the work of the "first-born among many brethren" and known as the "children of God" (Romans 8:29, 30; Hebrews 2:11-13). Brotherhood signifies mutual responsibility and love, the full participation of all in the family of God, a sharing fully in the life of the church. Brotherhood carries the same meaning that koinonia bears.

Jesus Himself gave a new definition to the term. Brothers, sisters, parents are those who do the will of God (Mark 3:35), those who give first priority to the obligations of the new spiritual family. They serve one another in their needs, be it food, clothing, or mutual support (Matthew 25). Distinctive levels of honor or superiority are nonexistent in this brotherhood. There are distinctions in terms of gifts and functions, but not in terms of superiority and inferiority. "Neither be called masters, for you have one master, the Christ" . . . "and you are all brethren" (Matthew 23: 10, 8).

Two dangers which threaten the full development of the New Testament ideal of koinonia in the life of the church are individualism and institutionalism. Individualism is an exaggerated sense of personal importance and responsibility which leads to neglect of brotherhood aspects of life in the body of Christ. Its characteristics include the tendency to go ahead on one's own, refusing to heed the counsel and warnings of the brotherhood, insisting on one's own rights rather than the well-being of the community, and the inclination to self-centeredness. Individualism perverts legitimate personal responsibility before God and the authentic dimensions of personal encounter with the Spirit of Christ, transforming it into a spirit of self-aggrandizement.

On the other hand, church structures which make it difficult for individuals to share fully in responsibility for the life of the Christian community deny the true nature of the body of Christ. Structures which relegate responsibility into the hands of a few, no matter if they are congregational or intercongregational, only encourage passive participation and loss of interest in brotherhood welfare by the members.

It is not a matter of either individual responsibility or institutional seriousness, but ordering both in accordance with the communitarian nature of the people of God. Institutions should serve the purposes of the church without entering into conflict with the fundamental nature of the church and its mission. The solution to the problem of individualism in the body of Christ is the presence of the Spirit of Christ, who enables us to "be subject to one another out of reverence for Christ" (Ephesians 5:21) and "through love be servants of one another" (Galatians 5:13). In the community of Jesus the problem of individualism is overcome through authentic relationships of mutual responsibility. The problem of institutionalism is overcome through authentic interpersonal relationships which are direct and fraternal.

Koinonia and renewal

Koinonia in the church has often been threatened and sometimes even destroyed by unbrotherly economic practices. Jesus warned that it would be very difficult for a rich man to enter the kingdom (Luke 18:25). He also said that anxiety about possessions is an attitude which may be expected among pagans, but is certainly not proper among His followers (Matthew 6:32). Paul gives the impression that one of the elements which contributed to division in the Corinthian congregation was economic differences within the brotherhood (1 Corinthians 11). He also points out that in the Christian community "the love of money is the root of all evils" (1 Timothy 6:10). James warns against the temptation in the church to favor the rich (James 2).

Judging by the warnings which appear in the New Testament it seems that the temptation to materialism presented a greater threat to the integrity of the primitive church than the temptation to exercise coercive power and to employ violence. As Jesus so well perceived, possessions exercise a diabolical power over persons. A kind of general demonic pressure seems to exist which causes one to sacrifice even one's highest ethical values for money.

Since apostolic times, then, koinonia has been an experience, not a theological abstraction, for multitudes of Christians. In order to realize community, communication among the members of the body is fundamental. Fellowship becomes concrete when Christians meet together. Time is required to develop commonality. But in order for koinonia to function at a practical level the possibility of primary interpersonal relationship is a necessity.

In these small groups koinonia can take on deeper dimensions as persons get to know one another. They give and receive counsel in order to make ethical decisions. They help one another in mutual discipline. They discern and encourage the exercise of the gifts which the Spirit has given to the body. They sustain one another in the daily paths of discipleship. All of this is grounded in a common experience of the grace of God through Jesus Christ and made real by the Holy Spirit who dwells in their midst.

The Holy Spirit of God creates, deepens, and extends the experience of community in the church. In the experience of Pentecost we find the negation of Babel. Since Pentecost, communication within and through a community has become a new possibility. In the New Testament, the Holy Spirit usually was poured out upon groups of persons, be they the company of disciples or family groups. The Holy Spirit was rarely given to individuals alone, and even in these cases He was given for the edification of the body of Christ.

Koinonia is an essential element in the life of the church of Jesus Christ. It should, therefore, come as no surprise that throughout the history of the church those renewal movements which have been concerned to recover their radical character in Christ have always rediscovered this dimension of commonality. This has been true of the Waldensians, the Czech Brethren, the Swiss Brethren, the Quakers, the early Methodists, as well as some contemporary renewal movements.

Renewal is not merely a matter of imitating an ancient model of Christian community with a view to change. It is rather a question of rediscovering experimentally that koinonia which is the essence of the community of Jesus Christ.

3. THE CHURCH:
A COMMUNITY OF FORGIVENESS

The Christian church is more than individuals gathered around the common experience of personal forgiveness received directly from God. It is more than a functional community organized to carry out its mission efficiently. The church is essentially a community in which members communicate God's forgiveness to one another and thus experience reconciliation concretely and personally. Through forgiving relationships among His people God makes visible His forgiveness in the world.

As we realize the role of forgiveness we begin to understand the New Testament meaning of discipline. Evangelism is basically an invitation to discipleship within a community of disciples. Discipline in the church is the necessary continuation of the evangelizing process carried out within a forgiving community.

Forgiveness in the New Testament

The New Testament demonstrates that the message of forgiveness must find expression between particular persons in specific times and places. Forgiveness becomes concrete among men and women who need to be reconciled among themselves and with God.

The passages which refer to binding and loosing (Matthew 16:18, 19; 18:15-20) are the only passages in the Gospels where the word "church" *(ecclesia)* is used by

Jesus. This probably indicates that the church was understood basically as the community in which binding
and loosing occur. The parallel passage in John 20:21-25
speaks of forgiving and retaining sins. Where this process
does not take place the church has not been realized according to the fullest intention of Jesus. In carrying out
these actions, the church does so as God's representative.
This is the only situation in which the church is explicitly
authorized to act in God's behalf.

In reality the "rule of Christ," as the passage in
Matthew 18:15-20 has been traditionally called, is placed
in the context of an entire chapter which speaks of
forgiveness:

- Importance of repentance and simplicity as conditions for receiving forgiveness (1-4).
- Importance of avoiding offenses which may cause
the fall of a brother (5-11).
- Concern of God that all should experience
forgiveness (12-14).
- "Rule of Christ" (15-20).
- Importance of willingness to forgive without limits.
(21, 22).
- Importance of forgiving in order to experience
forgiveness (23-25).

The only petition in the Lord's Prayer which carries a
condition is the one asking for forgiveness (Matthew
6:12): "Forgive us our debts, *as we also have forgiven our
debtors.*" This is also the only phrase in the prayer which
requires additional comment, emphasizing again that
God's forgiveness is limited to those who forgive their
brothers and sisters (Matthew 6:14, 15). We find this condition repeated a number of times in the New Testament

(Matthew 18:35; Mark 11:25; Ephesians 4:32; Colossians 3:13). A person is incapable of receiving God's forgiveness and even unable to offer a valid act of worship without first being reconciled with brothers or sisters through forgiveness (Matthew 5:23, 24).

The same instructions (given in Matthew 18:15-20) concerning forgiveness in the Christian community are reiterated in the epistles: "Brethren, if a man is overtaken in any trespass, you who are spiritual should restore him in a spirit of gentleness. Look to yourself, lest you too be tempted. Bear one another's burdens, and so fulfil the law of Christ" (Galatians 6:1, 2). "My brethren, if any one among you wanders from the truth and someone brings him back, let him know that whoever brings back a sinner from the error of his way will save his soul from death and will cover a multitude of sins" (James 5:19, 20). (The last phrase is undoubtedly a citation from Proverbs 10:12: "Love covers all offenses." (See also 2 Timothy 2:24, 25.)

In the context of this forgiving or restoring activity of the church, Christ (or the Holy Spirit) is present where men and women meet together in His name. Christ Himself will be among the "two or three gathered" for the purpose of restoring some member of the body (Matthew 18:19, 20). To exercise the function of forgiving or retaining sins, Jesus gave the Holy Spirit to His disciples (John 20:22, 23). Other passages (John 14:26 and 16:12-14) also point out that the church can count on the presence of the Spirit in the community's process of moral discernment which is always a part of binding and loosing.

This brief review of New Testament passages concerning forgiveness and restoration underscores that forgiveness is not secondary or marginal to the essential activity of the church. Where forgiving persons exercise discipline the church lives.

Discipline in the community of Jesus

The New Testament does not use "discipline" strictly to refer to the process of moral discernment through which members can be forgiven and restored in the community of Christ. In our use of the term we refer to that process called binding and loosing in the New Testament rather than to what the word has come to mean through the accumulation of meanings related to the exercise of ecclesiastical discipline in the church's history. While the terms binding and loosing were apparently clear to Jesus' hearers, their meaning is hidden to twentieth-century readers.

To bind meant to withhold pardon, to retain (sins) and, therefore, to exclude from the fellowship of the community. To loose meant to absolve, to pardon, to forgive (sins). This meaning of binding and loosing becomes clear when one compares the parallel passages in Luke 17:3 and John 20:23 The general context of Matthew 18 which deals with forgiveness supports this interpretation.

But binding and loosing also carried another meaning. To bind meant to forbid, or to make obligatory, or to order a certain course of moral behavior. To loose meant to permit, or to leave a person free to make an ethical choice among various alternatives. This was the way in which these terms were used by the Jewish rabbis of Jesus' time. In their interpretations of the law of Israel they bound or loosed (forbade or permitted) certain moral alternatives, depending on the nature of each case. When Jesus used these terms, whose meaning had been fixed by their rabbinical usage, He was in effect granting to His disciples the moral authority which until then had been the prerogative only of the great teachers of Israel. This dimension of the meaning of binding and loosing is emphasized in Matthew 16:19.

Both sets of meanings are present in Matthew 18:15-20. Restoration through repentance and forgiveness is the principal theme of verses 15-17, where second person singular verb forms describe interpersonal relationships. But verses 18-20 treat the question of moral discernment. Plural verbs suggest authorization to make certain moral decisions in the church and may well have a broader scope than the immediate case of discipline under consideration. Although they may appear to be two distinct matters, they are closely related in the Christian community.

1. The process of restoring brothers and sisters through repentance and forgiveness presupposes a common moral basis. The ethical norms by which sin is recognized are known and shared mutually, thus providing criteria for evaluating offense.

2. The process of conversation aimed at restoration is the best way to clarify, to test, and then either to confirm or to change community ethics. This process leads to a new experience in discernment of God's will and is the path to restoration and reconciliation among brothers and sisters.

So forgiveness and moral discernment are not different meanings of binding and loosing but rather two sides of the same coin. Discipline from a gospel perspective includes the process of moral discernment with a view to making ethical decisions in the community, as well as the personal dimension of forgiveness and restoration through brotherly address and repentance. To exercise discipline without the accompanying process of moral discernment is to run the risk of becoming legalistic, inflexible, and mechanical. On the other hand, moral discernment without reference to the personal dimension of brotherly counsel, forgiveness, and restoration will become cold, impersonal, and academic.

Purpose of discipline determines form

According to the New Testament passages already noted, the purpose of discipline in the gospel perspective will always be the restoration and reconciliation of the offending member. This purpose will determine the forms in which discipline is exercised in the community.

1. The path to reconciliation is always personal and should be taken in the spirit of humility (Galatians 6:1, 2). What is really important in the instructions given in Matthew 18:15-17 is not that there will always be a process involving three steps, but rather that the first steps always be personal—"between you and him alone" and "take one or two brothers along with you."

Taking this procedure seriously goes a long way toward eliminating situations in which gossip and character defamation prosper. Besides promoting direct relationships and mutual confidence, this approach guards against an impersonal, puritanical moralism. Through serious and mutual conversation the Lord's will for His disciples will be made known. Any norm unable to survive such confrontation in the presence of the Spirit no longer serves the best interests of the community.

On the other hand, this form of exercising discipline

avoids the pitfall of leaving each individual at liberty to make ethical choices alone. Ultimately the member is answerable to the community for the moral decisions which he makes. Discipline in the gospel perspective is sufficiently flexible to consider each case in its context without becoming permissive.

2. In accord with the communitarian nature of the church, the entire congregation shares responsibility for exercise of gospel discipline. The initiative in this process of course belongs to any brother who becomes conscious of an offense (Matthew 18:15). The words "against you" are not found in the better manuscripts of the New Testament nor do we find this limitation in Luke 17:3, Galatians 6:1, 2 or James 5:19, 20. It is his obligation as a brother, rather than the feeling that he has been sinned against, that causes one member of the community to approach another who may have sinned. On the other hand, Matthew 5:23-25 assigns the initiative to the person who has committed the offense, just as soon as he becomes conscious of it.

So the initiative for restoring sound interpersonal relationships within the community becomes the responsibility of all—the offended, the offender, or any brother or sister who may know of the offense. There are no indications in the New Testament that responsibility for initiative belongs particularly to the set-apart ministry. It may be assumed that congregational leaders will be interested in the proper exercise of fraternal discipline with a view to restoration and reconciliation in the brotherhood. But to conceive of the elder, pastor, teacher, or deacon as the one who normally or exclusively takes responsibility for the exercise of discipline in the congregation is contrary to the spirit of the New Testament.

3. The restoration and reconciliation of the offending brother is the only legitimate purpose for the exercise of discipline in a gospel perspective. Of course, other reasons are adduced: concern for church purity, desire to protect the reputation of the church before the world, wish to bear witness to the high demands of God's righteousness through the vindication of His justice, attempt to safeguard the church against the danger of relativizing or losing its high standards.

Although these concerns are real, they are secondary; the New Testament does not emphasize them. While the church is often concerned about maintaining its public image, the New Testament speaks of a concern for restoration and reconciliation in the community through sincere repentance and healing forgiveness.

There is a sense, however, in which the sin of an unrepentant member may become a "leaven" which affects the entire body (1 Corinthians 5). The persistent disobedience of individuals within the church which goes unchallenged by the community may become a collective fault shared by the entire body. Unless we become agents of our offending brother's restoration, he may well become an agent of our collective guilt.

Authority for exercise of gospel discipline

If we take seriously the claims of the New Testament, we must recognize that the authority with which Christ has invested the church is parallel to the authority which He claimed for Himself. Jesus scandalized the Jews by the way in which He claimed for Himself a unique relationship with the Father. However, Jesus went on to declare to His disciples, "As the Father has sent me, even so I send you" (John 20:21). But even more offensive to the Jews was Jesus' claim to be able to forgive men their sins (Mark 2:7; Luke 7:48-50). However, this is precisely the task with which Jesus later charged His disciples. He granted to them (and to us as well) the same power to forgive sins that He had claimed for Himself.

This is the scandal which shook up the Pharisees and which generally shakes up Protestants, too, as they begin to grasp its significance. Reacting to abuses inherent in the traditional Roman Catholic penitential practice, Protestants have declared for centuries that "God alone can forgive sins" and that believers receive assurance of their forgiveness not from the lips of another man, but from a voice speaking in the depths of their own souls. The way in which this long-standing debate between Catholics and Protestants has been formulated makes it difficult for us to believe that men and women can be authorized in God's new community to make binding and loosing decisions that God will honor.

For the Jews it was a Christological scandal—God has elected to forgive and restore men and women through the Man Jesus. For us it is an ecclesiological scandal— God has elected to forgive and restore men and women in and through His new community. The incarnation has always been a scandal: the form which God has chosen to do His work among humankind has been through the carpenter of Nazareth who commissioned a group of or- dinary people—fishermen and tax collectors—to forgive sins and to restore men and women to wholeness.

This in no sense means that the church may use its authority arbitrarily. For this task the church receives the power of the Holy Spirit. The gift of the Spirit is directly related to the commission to forgive sins (John 20:21-23). To make decisions in ethical matters the church may count on the Spirit who will guide into truth and will reveal the meaning of Jesus' words and deeds (John 14:26; 16:12-14). Judging from New Testament emphasis, the fundamental work of the Holy Spirit is guiding the church in its task of moral discernment. Prophecy, witness, inner conviction, and enablement to follow Jesus are all important, but subordinate, aspects of His activity.

Modern Protestants have often understood the promise of Christ's presence where two or three are gathered in His name to refer to the efficacy of prayer or to the spiritual presence of Christ in the gathered congregation. One often hears an appeal to this promise when poor attendance at meetings might otherwise discourage churchgoers. But according to its original context in Matthew 18:19, 20, the presence of Christ Himself among His disciples is promised for the divinely authorized process of moral discernment to make real forgiveness and restoration.

It is surely no accident that the commission to bind and loose in Matthew 16 follows immediately after Peter's confession that Jesus is the Messiah. This confession of Christ's lordship is the basis for the authority which Christ granted His church. The church is that community in which Jesus is confessed and obeyed as Messiah and Lord. The authorization is the seal of divine approval conferred upon their confession. For that reason men and women in this community are authorized to speak to one another words of moral counsel, forgiveness, and restoration in God's name.

Deformations and misunderstandings

The radical essence of the New Testament understanding of discipline has not been appreciated generally because of deformations and misunderstandings which surrounded it in church history. The list which follows is representative.

1. Sometimes we refrain from taking part in our brother's or sister's struggle against temptation, alleging acceptance, respect for personal differences, love. If the only alternative were a traditional puritanical approach to discipline, such respect may be understandable, but abandoning the member to personal struggles, guilt, uncertainties, and misguided moral decisions is not brotherly love in any sense. In the community of Christ, love never abandons a member.

2. Another excuse stems from false modesty. "Who am I to tell my brother that he is sinning, because I, too, am certainly far from perfect?" To justify nonintervention one sometimes hears the example of the beam and the mote (or the log and speck, as a newer translation puts it). But when Jesus used this example His conclusion was opposite. A person with a beam should recognize that it is there, and then take it out so that he can see well enough to remove the small foreign body from the eye of another (Matthew 7:3-5). Even if it is true that we are all sinners, Jesus does not base our obligation to forgive and to reconcile on the supposed absence of sin from our experience. He says that those who are called to mediate forgiveness and restoration are precisely those who have experienced forgiveness themselves (Matthew 6:12).

3. Occasionally we appeal to the excuse of maturity. "If my brother has sinned, I have certainly not taken

offense. With my emotional stability I'm able to overlook his faults. There's no need to bother him or others because of it." Such an excuse comes from an inadequate interpretation of the phrase "if your brother sins *against you.*" Our motivation for helping a member dare not be our personal sense of having been offended, but rather, our obligation to the person as a fellow member. Paul reminds us that it is precisely the more mature ("you who are spiritual") who should take the initiative in the restoration of one who is sinning (Galatians 6:1).

4. Sometimes we excuse nonintervention because the member may become to us as a Gentile and a tax collector should he resist our efforts to restore him. A modern spirit of tolerance among us rebels at such exclusivism. This objection arises out of a misunderstanding of what "let him be to you as a Gentile and tax collector" really means. According to the spirit of the New Testament, this implies that we must recognize that an erstwhile member has become the object of our evangelistic concern. It means that we will shower upon the person the same kind of love and concern which the community showed before he confessed Jesus Christ as Lord. Far from being punitive, this represents a redemptive attitude toward the member who has said "no" to the lordship of Jesus Christ. It is the only way left to love responsibly.

Recovery leads to thanksgiving

We have outlined what it means to be a community in which forgiveness, restoration to wholeness, and reconciliation are experienced according to the vision of Jesus. But this vision has so easily become deformed in the life of the Christian church. The price we are paying for neglect of this essential function of the church is incalculably high. Our disobedience means that we are no longer the church in which the Holy Spirit is at work *in the way Christ promised.*

Congregational life becomes increasingly formal and its true significance escapes as an illusion. More and more we feel that what we do when we gather together lacks authenticity. We do not really get to those issues concerning our common life in Christ which basically matter. We are not able to discern together with clarity the will of God in order to repent and forgive and restore one another with authority. According to Jesus, this is a fundamental function of the Spirit of God in the church. According to the New Testament, this is the function which defines the existence of the church.

The absence of this essential function of the Holy Spirit from the church causes us to emphasize other functions and manifestations of the Holy Spirit's presence in the body of Christ. Although these are good and edifying and appropriate and necessary, they are not equally indispensable for the church's life. In some churches these secondary activities of the Spirit include such things as Christian education and social services. In other congregations one finds a certain concentration on some of the more exciting visible and even ecstatic manifestations of the work of the Holy Spirit in the community. But in both cases, this somewhat exclusive concentration on part of the Spirit's ministry indicates that the real center around which the community of the Spirit is constituted has been lost. Recovery of this central function of the Holy Spirit in the church would permit us to receive and exercise with thanksgiving *all* of the rich gamut of spiritual gifts.

4. THE CHURCH:
A COMMUNITY OF GIFTS

The New Testament epistles serve as windows to observe the intimate life of Christian communities during the first century. They were communities experiencing a rich variety of gifts which the Holy Spirit poured out for their edification. The gospel was a contemporary reality in their common life. They gathered together expectantly. They worshipped God in singing and with joyful praise.

Early Christians gathered to receive counsel from one another, keeping their daily moral decisions in line with the Spirit and words of Jesus. Some of the worshipers occasionally offered praise in unknown tongues, giving testimony to the presence of God's Spirit. Others shared convictions which God had revealed, helping the community to discern the will of God in their situation. Although there were prophets and teachers and pastors, the meetings do not seem to have been oriented around any one particular person. All present participated in celebration, instruction, and mutual edification. Primary passages which describe the place of the Spirit's gifts in the common life of the church are Romans 12; 1 Corinthians 12 to 14; and Ephesians 4.

Jesus is Lord
One of the first things which impresses a careful reader is the ethical context in which the lists of spiritual gifts are

placed. In Romans 12 the list of the gifts of the Spirit is set within the framework of moral teaching. Life within the community of the Spirit of God requires nothing less than a literal transformation "by the renewal of your mind" (12:2). The Greek term *metamorphosis* is translated "transformed," meaning a radical moral change. Only an experience of repentance will permit us to know the will of God and live up to His expectations.

The ethical stance described in the rest of Romans 12 finds its inspiration in the Sermon on the Mount. The humility described in verse 3 reminds us of the Spirit of Jesus described in Philippians 2 and reflected in the Beatitudes. The genuine love described in verse 9 and the counsel to share with those in need (verse 13) remind us of the teachings of Jesus, as well as the practices of Jesus and His disciples. In verses 14-21 we find a repetition of Jesus' teachings concerning vengeance and love for the enemy (Matthew 5:38-48).

In Ephesians 4 we find the same ethical concerns. "To lead a life worthy of the calling to which you have been called" implies interpersonal relationships characterized by lowliness, meekness, patience, and love (verses 1, 2). This is the same ethical stance described in the Beatitudes (Matthew 5). Here also we find an appeal to "be renewed in the spirit of your minds, and put on the new nature" (verses 23, 24). Again, this is radical repentance. The new lifestyle includes speaking the truth (verse 25), resisting the temptation to anger (verses 26, 31), and sharing one's goods with those who are needy (verse 28). All of these elements occur in the Sermon on the Mount (Matthew 5:33, 22; 6:19, 20).

In 1 Corinthians 12 the two lists of spiritual gifts (verses

4-8, 27-31) are preceded by the concern that Jesus be recognized as Lord (verse 3). This is possible only through the activity of the Holy Spirit within the community. The work par excellence of the Spirit is to insure that Jesus is truly confessed as Lord in His church.

All of the gifts of the Spirit are for the welfare of the church. Through their exercise the church is built up. All of the Spirit's gifts to the church should be awaited, received with thanksgiving, and exercised for the glory of God within the body of Christ. The gifts are not valid alone. Their authenticity should not be accepted automatically. All gifts within the church must be measured against the lordship of Jesus Christ.

To confess that Jesus is Lord necessarily implies submitting to the reign of Christ, living in accord with that style of life which characterizes His kingdom. When a spiritual gift is exercised in a way which denies the lordship of Jesus, that gift is revealed as spurious. Authentic spiritual gifts will be recognized by their conformity to Jesus Christ and His kingdom.

The fact that the lordship of Jesus is normative for determining the authenticity of spiritual gifts explains why Paul places his lists of the Spirit's gifts (in Romans and Ephesians) within a context of ethical teachings which reflect the Sermon on the Mount. The Sermon on the Mount is a résumé of life in the kingdom where Jesus is Lord. And this is the life manifest in that community where an authentic flowering of gifts has occurred.

We are one body

Another thing which impresses the biblical reader is the way the figure of the body and its members is used in each passage. In Romans 12:4 to 6a Paul emphasizes the fundamental unity of the church within which the diversity of spiritual gifts is manifest. Romans 12:3 implies that each member of the congregation has received some spiritual gift. There are a great variety of functions, but these need not pose a threat to the unity of the church. The members "though many, are one body in Christ" and furthermore, they are "individually members one of another" (Romans 12:5).

In 1 Corinthians 12 the figure of the body and its members demonstrates Paul's thesis: "There are varieties of gifts, but the same Spirit" (verse 4). The church, Paul says, by its nature is a body made up of diverse elements. The church exists when Jews and Greeks, slave and free (verse 13), male and female (Galatians 3:28), and all of those groups separated by "the dividing wall" (Ephesians 2:14) are formed into one body through baptism in the power of "one Spirit" (verse 13). On the basis of this fundamental unity, recognizing and encouraging the many authentic manifestations of the Spirit in the church becomes possible. This variety in the church responds to the gracious initiative of God (verse 18). All of the gifts, the least desirable as well as those with the greatest appeal, are indispensable (verse 22). This is true because all gifts and persons are essential to the healthy functioning of the church. Unity comes through deep relationships of mutual responsibility which characterize the body of Christ (verses 25b-27).

This aspect of the fundamental nature of the church is noted with even greater clarity in Ephesians 4. Direct references to the body are limited to verses 4, 15, and 16, where we find the same emphasis as in Romans 12 and 1

Corinthians 12. There is one body whose essential purpose is realized as members complement one another by the rich variety of their gifts. Two new elements in this text contribute to our understanding of the theological significance of the diversity of the gifts.

1. Paul says in Ephesians 4:8 that the work of Christ consists of giving gifts to men. This is an aspect of the work of the glorified Christ. The Lord who gives this variety of gifts to men is the One "who also ascended far above all the heavens, that he might fill all things" (Ephesians 4:10). Hebrews 2:3, 4 points out that the saving work of Christ is attested "by gifts of the Holy Spirit distributed according to his own will." So the distribution of gifts is a part of the saving work of the glorified Christ, the certification of His victory.

2. The phrases, "the equipment of the saints . . . for building up the body of Christ" (4:12), "the fullness of Christ" (4:13), and "the whole body . . . when each part is working properly . . . upbuilds itself in love" (4:16), all refer to the correct and harmonious relationship of the gifts enumerated in verse 11. The body of Christ is fully present to the extent that all of the gifts are exercised for the common good. To interpret verse 13, for example, in terms of the maturing process of an individual Christian is out of harmony with the sense of the entire passage. "Mature manhood" and "the fullness of Christ" both describe the church in which the various gifts are divinely coordinated.

Therefore, we note that when the apostles say that "to each" is given a gift (Romans 12:3; 1 Corinthians 7:7, 12:7; Ephesians 4:7; 1 Peter 4:10), they are not merely describing an important characteristic of the first-century church. They are pointing to a normative element in its life. The church will be fully the body of Christ to the extent that all of the gifts which are given it through the Spirit are recognized and exercised in the community. Plurality (more than one person in the congregation may exercise a particular gift) and universality (every member receives at least one gift) of spiritual gifts in the community are integral to church life.

The gifts of the Spirit

The New Testament uses an extensive vocabulary to refer to the gifts of the Spirit. In Romans 12 they are simply called "gifts" (charismata) (verse 6). In 1 Corinthians 12 they are called "spiritual gifts" (verse 1); "gifts" (charismata) (verses 4, 9, 30-31); "service" (diaconia) (verse 5); "working" (verse 6); and "manifestations of the Spirit" (verse 7). In Ephesians 4 the terms "grace" (charis) and "gift" are used (verses 7, 8).

The passages under consideration mention some 18 gifts or gifted persons given by the Spirit to the church. Prophecy occurs in all four lists. The teaching function appears in three of the lists. Others are found in two lists, while some are included only once. This implies that these listings, both individually and taken together, are not exhaustive but representative of the rich variety of the Spirit's gifts to the church. To know exactly how each gift was exercised in the primitive church is impossible, but gifts can be distinguished in general terms.

1. *Utterance of wisdom* (1 Corinthians 12:8) is the capacity to discern and exposite the Word of God in a way that moves the community on toward maturity in Christ.

2. *Utterance of knowledge* (1 Corinthians 12:8) is the

capacity to teach in a more elemental form the rudiments of faith. (See Hebrews 6:1, where the writer contrasts elementary teaching with maturity.) Both these gifts are certainly related to the function of teacher.

3. *Faith* (1 Corinthians 12:9) is the courage to undertake seemingly difficult tasks which would appear to exceed human calculations and resources. Judging from 1 Corinthians 13:2 this appears to be the kind of faith which moves mountains.

4. *Gifts of healing* (1 Corinthians 12:9, 28) relate to the particular activity which identified Jesus as the Messiah according to the pattern of the suffering servant described by the prophet Isaiah (Matthew 8:17). Similarly, the exercise of this gift in the church will serve to identify the community of the servant Messiah.

5. *Working of miracles* (1 Corinthians 12:10, 28) refers to works of extraordinary power which give evidence to the activity of the Holy Spirit in the messianic community (compare Galatians 3:5 and Acts 10:38).

6. *Prophecy* (1 Corinthians 12:10; Romans 12:6) and *prophets* (1 Corinthians 12:28; Ephesians 4:11) refer to men and women who speak in God's name under the inspiration of His Spirit. One of their functions seems to have been understanding and explaining teachings from the Scriptures through the enlightenment of the Spirit (1 Peter 1:10-12). This gift appears to flower in the era of the Spirit (Acts 2:17, 18; 11:27).

7. *Ability to distinguish between spirits* (1 Corinthians 12:10), as the capacity in the church to determine the origin of spiritual manifestations—from God or from demons—is of fundamental importance in a time when such manifestations abound.

8. *Various kinds of tongues* (1 Corinthians 12:10, 28).

9. *Interpretation of tongues* (1 Corinthians 12:10, 30). Glossolalia consists of the emission of unintelligible sounds only made rationally meaningful by one who exercises the gift of interpretation. According to the New Testament glossolalia occurred in Corinth, Caesarea, Ephesus, and possibly Jerusalem. The tongues at Pentecost represent a similar phenomenon (Acts 2:4, 11, 13), although with certain differences (Acts 2:6-8). Paul calls them "tongues of angels" (1 Corinthians 13:1). Contrary to the charisma of prophecy whose main purpose is edification, glossolalia primarily witnesses to the presence of the Spirit in the church. Of course tongues do edify the one who speaks (1 Corinthians 14:4) and prophecy also witnesses to the Holy Spirit's presence (1 Corinthians 14:25).

10. *Apostles* (1 Corinthians 12:28; Ephesians 4:11). In addition to the Twelve, together with Paul, Barnabas, and James, this designation probably also includes a wider circle of missioners who, under the impulse of the Holy Spirit, evangelized and founded new Christian communities (Romans 16:7; 2 Corinthians 8:23).

11. *Teachers* (1 Corinthians 12:29; Ephesians 4:11) and *teaching* (Romans 12:7). In the community in Antioch the ministry of teacher was closely associated with that of the prophets (Acts 13:1). Their function was strategic in that they helped to conserve the sense of identity of the Christian communities through the conservation and interpretation of their tradition. James suggests that this may be one of the more dangerous charismas. For that reason there should not be too many (James 3:1 following).

12. *Helpers* (1 Corinthians 12:28) and *service* (Romans

12:7) refer to the fundamental practice of serving those in need in Christian love.

13. *Administrators* (1 Corinthians 12:28) and *he who gives aid* (or presides) (Romans 12:8) refer to giving direction to the life and service of the Christian community. This function seems to be subordinated to those of service and teaching. The form which the presiding function takes within the community is determined by Jesus, who lived among His disciples as One who served (Luke 22:27).

14. *He who exhorts* (Romans 12:8): to console or to encourage.

15. *He who contributes* (Romans 12:8): to share one's goods with others.

16. *He who does acts of mercy* (Romans 12:8): to succor those who are in need. The last three gifts are undoubtedly interrelated.

17. *Evangelists* (Ephesians 4:11) are itinerant preachers of the good news about the kingdom of God and the Messiah (Acts 8:12).

18. *Pastors* (Ephesians 4:11) were charged to care for members of the community as the "flock of God" (1 Peter 5:2). As a reference to a particular function in the Christian community, this is the only time that the term appears in the New Testament, although the elders of the church in Ephesus are charged to "take heed . . . to all the flock" of which the Holy Spirit had made them guardians (Acts 20:28).

Love and gifts of the Spirit

In each of the principal passages in which Paul treats the subject of the gifts of the Spirit, he also issues a call to genuine love for one another (Romans 12: 9, 10; 1 Corinthians 13; Ephesians 4:2). The relationship between love and the spiritual gifts is spelled out most fully in 1 Corinthians 13, where love is related to, but distinguished from, the gifts of the Spirit. Love is poured out upon God's people together with the spiritual gifts, but it is superior to all of these. Apart from love, none of the charismas will prove to be useful. In contrast to all of the gifts of the Spirit, love is intrinsic to the kingdom which knows no end. In the consummation of the kingdom other gifts will become obsolete, but love alone will never end.

Norms for measuring authenticity

The lordship of Christ as a norm against which the authenticity of the exercise of spiritual gifts can be measured has already been noted. Paul offers a second standard: edification. The theme of this upbuilding— encouragement and consolation of the Christian community—runs like a refrain through the passages in 1 Corinthians 14: 3-5, 12, 19, 26, 31 and Ephesians 4:12. Every personal desire for self-realization or individual spiritual satisfaction must be subordinated to the criteria of that which contributes to the upbuilding of the body of Christ.

Toward an understanding of spiritual gifts

The lists of spiritual gifts or ministries given in the epistles do not pretend to be complete. The sovereign Lord of the church is the One who gives gifts to men and He will give to His people all of the gifts that they need to function fully as His body. The church can be assured that the Spirit of God will provide all of the gifts that are required in any particular situation.

Numerous attempts to classify the gifts of the Spirit have proved to be of limited usefulness.

1. Sometimes distinction is made between gifts and ministries or functions. Gifts are understood as unpredictable activities inspired by the Spirit. Human ability can neither determine nor control their operation. Although a great blessing to the church, gifts defy attempts to organize or ordain their contribution to the community's life. On the other hand, ministries are understood as regular and ordained functions usually recognized through ordination. Such a way of classifying gifts seems inconsistent. The laying on of hands as an act of ordination was used to commission the seven (Acts 6:6) and Paul (Acts 13:3), but hands were also laid on entire congregations (Acts 8:17; 19:6). In the latter case they spoke in tongues and prophesied. When classifying the gifts of the Spirit into ordainable and non-ordainable categories we find that the dividing line becomes elusive.

2. Sometimes spiritual gifts are understood to be experienced by any member of the community at any time. Temporary and often sensational, they are contrasted with more permanent gifts which are often formally recognized. This attempt to classify gifts clashes with texts like 1 Corinthians 12:7, 11, 27; Romans 12:3; Ephesians 4:7, where all gifts without distinction are described as particular gifts granted to each one. The New Testament understanding of spiritual gifts in the church is that of charismatic plurality and universality; to classify some ministries as special seems ill-advised.

3. Sometimes a distinction has been made between

charismatic and non-charismatic gifts. Charisma, a term used by sociologists of religion, has passed over into secular usage to describe public figures with that extra something. The same phenomenon is noted in certain religious movements, where leaders are granted authority by virtue of their charisma. This use of the term underscores more spectacular elements. But in 1 Corinthians 12 and Romans 12 there is no gift which is not charismatic. Of course, some gifts may be more attractive than others and some are for leaders while others are for helpers, but all are charismas.

Another source contributing to the current definition of charismatic are certain renewal movements which have recovered some of the elements of classic Pentecostalism. Since designations such as neo-Pentecostal have not been fully acceptable, the term charismatic movement has come to be accepted. This usage of charismatic is associated principally with the gifts of prophecy, healings, miracles, tongues and their interpretation. When we say that Christians who exercise one or more of these five gifts are charismatic, while those who exercise other spiritual gifts are not, we contradict 1 Corinthians 12 to 14. All gifts are charismatic and all should be submitted to certain controls within the community. Extra-rational gifts are not necessarily the more excellent ones.

4. Sometimes distinctions are made between spiritual gifts judged to be natural and those which are supernatural, or suprarational. But insofar as all of the spiritual gifts are gifts of God's grace—charismata—they are beyond nature, they are all supernatural. For their exercise in the body of Christ all require the supernatural grace of God. Natural gifts are not sufficient. Charismata are needed.

For example, when a congregation attempts to discern leadership gifts the temptation sometimes comes to lay hands on a natural leader or a successful executive in the congregation. But the fact that a person is a natural leader is not a sign that he exercises the spiritual gift of presiding. In fact, it may well mean that he does not have this gift. It requires a supernatural gift to preside in the community of the Lord who has taken the form of a servant. Being a success at IBM or General Motors is an altogether different thing.

5. Finally, we are tempted to classify the gifts of the Spirit in terms of importance. This practice is based on the list of gifts in 1 Corinthians 12:28, where the terminology seems to indicate an order of precedence. It is possible to arrange them in terms of a certain logical order, but it would be precarious to establish a general order of importance on the basis of only eight out of an indefinite number of gifts. It is not wise to rank the gifts of the Spirit. All gifts of the Spirit to the church are important. This importance is most noticeable when the gift is absent. When the internal social situation in a congregation is chaotic, probably the most important gift would be found in one able to moderate among the factions and reestablish order. For a floundering church which has lost contact with its historical roots, possibly the most important gift comes in a teacher capable of interpreting its past, helping it to recover its reason for existence in the present, and developing a vision for the future. Or for such a church perhaps a prophet with a word from the Lord to reorient its life is most needed. In a church grounded on the shoals of traditionalism and ecclesiastical rigidity, perhaps the most important gift is

tongues which bear witness to the presence of the Holy Spirit living and working in their midst.

The intention of the Holy Spirit is to create community—a community in which the fruits of His ministry are abundantly evident, a community on which the spiritual gifts are poured out to reveal the potential of a church living in anticipation of the coming kingdom already inaugurated by its Lord.

5. THE CHURCH:
A COMMUNITY OF PEACE

The term "peace" in its principal forms occurs about 100 times in the New Testament. In his sermon in the house of Cornelius, Peter pointed out that the substance of God's message to Israel is "the gospel of peace by Jesus Christ" (Acts 10:36). Paul referred several times to the good news as the "gospel of peace" (Ephesians 2:17; 6:15; Romans 10:15). In Ephesians 2 he points out that the fundamental work of Jesus Christ is the creation of a new community of peace.

Peace occupies a prominent place in the Scripture and is basic to understanding the gospel. The Scriptures tell us that God is a God of peace; that Jesus Christ is Lord of peace (the prophet called the expected Messiah the Prince of Peace); that the Holy Spirit is the Spirit of peace; that the kingdom of God is justice, peace, and joy in the Holy Spirit; that the new sons of God are peacemakers; that the gospel is good news of peace. The peace of God is at the center of the life we live and the message we proclaim as disciples of Jesus Christ.

In what sense can the good news of the saving activity of God in favor of humankind be called the gospel of peace? In our search for the answer we should expect little help from the history of the church during the past seventeen or eighteen centuries. With the passing of the centuries so many extraneous elements have entered the church that it has become difficult, and in some cases impossible, to understand that the gospel of Jesus Christ is centered around peace. It can be admitted, of course, that peace of mind and inner tranquillity are among the benefits of the gospel. But it is almost out of the question for many to understand restored relationships among men and women within a new messianic community as essential to the gospel.

As a result of interaction with surrounding culture, the life and self-understanding of the church have tended to undergo modifications. That is why the church is obliged to constantly refer to its roots in Jesus Christ. In order to renew itself it must leap back over its accumulated deformations and reorient itself in the incarnation. One of the more flagrant deformations relates to concepts of peace which have prevailed in much of the church's history.

Peace in the biblical tradition

It should be remembered that Jesus and the apostles were Jews. First-century political power found its center in Rome, while Greece exercised intellectual leadership. Although the Roman colonial presence was felt in Palestine, and although the Greek language was used for popular communication (the New Testament was written in Greek), Jesus and His disciples were fundamentally Hebrews in their character and thought forms. They stood within the ancient tradition of the Hebrew prophets (Matthew 5:12). When Jesus and Peter and Paul speak of peace and declare that the good news of God's salvation is the gospel of peace, they use the term not as would their Roman and Greek contemporaries, but in the Hebrew sense of *shalom*.

Shalom is a broad concept, essential to the Hebrew understanding of relationship between people and God. It covers human welfare, health, and well-being in both spiritual and material aspects. It describes a condition of well-being resulting from sound relationships among people and between people and God. According to the prophets, true peace reigned in Israel when justice (or righteousness) prevailed, when the common welfare was assured, when people were treated with equality and respect, when salvation flourished according to the social order determined by God in the covenant which He had established with His people. In fact, the prophet understood that God's covenant with Israel was "a covenant of life and peace" (Malachi 2:5).

On the other hand, when there was greed for unjust gain, when judges could be bought for a price, when there was not equal opportunity for all, when suffering was caused by social and economic oppression, then there was no peace, even though false prophets insisted to the contrary (Jeremiah 6:13, 14).

For the Hebrews, peace was not merely the absence of armed conflict. Rather, shalom was assured by the prevalence of conditions which contribute to human well-being in all its dimensions. Not mere tranquillity of spirit or serenity of mind, peace had to do with harmonious relationships between God and His people. It had to do with social relationships characterized by justice. Peace resulted when people lived together according to God's intention. Peace, justice, and salvation are synonymous terms for general well-being created by right social relationships.

To the biblical writers peace is the gift of God to His

people. Above all, shalom described the messianic
kingdom which would be inaugurated. Giving expression
to this hope, the prophet Isaiah wrote:

> *How beautiful upon the mountains are the feet*
> *of him who brings good tidings,*
> *who publishes peace,*
> *who brings good tidings of good,*
> *who publishes salvation,*
> *who says to Zion, "Your God reigns."—Isaiah 52:7.*

The parallel lines in this verse are synonymous. Jesus
and Peter and Paul, too, used the term peace in the
Hebrew sense of shalom. Jesus promised His disciples
more than psychological encouragement to bolster their
spirits for difficult times ahead when He said, "Peace I
leave with you; my peace I give to you; not as the world
gives do I give to you" (John 14:27).

Peace was the customary word of greeting and farewell
among the Jews. But more, it means wholeness of body
and spirit and that perfect felicity and liberation which are
the gifts of the Messiah. All of this Jesus bestowed on His
disciples, anticipating that life of well-being and salvation
in the peace of the new community of the Spirit.

The Holy Spirit makes it possible for men and women
to live according to God's new covenant in right
relationships (justice), mutual understanding, respect,
love, and peace. Peace is a gift which the Spirit bestows
not upon only a few individuals, but upon all of the
members of Christ's body so that they might live in community as God has intended.

This concept of peace does not negate personal peace

which provides individuals with inner confidence and spiritual security. But a holistic understanding underscores that biblical peace is much more inclusive than the church has generally imagined. Shalom places the individual within the new community of the Spirit, where the fruits of the Spirit abound, where the gifts of the Spirit are received with thanksgiving, and where salvation which the Spirit makes possible is experienced with joy.

Peace among the Greeks

Early in its experience, the primitive church began to cross political and cultural boundaries. The movement which had been nurtured within Judaism was carried by the missionary vitality of first-century believers throughout the Roman empire. Christian missionaries confronted the Greco-Roman world with the gospel of peace. The Greeks, of course, had their own term for peace—*eirene*. However, its meaning was considerably different from shalom.

Among the Greeks, peace was primarily a state or a condition, in contrast to the dynamic meaning of shalom with its emphasis on right interpersonal relationships. Eirene meant a state of rest or tranquillity, defined by absence of conflict rather than by positive social relationships. The Stoics, for example, understood peace mainly as mental and spiritual harmony or inner order manifest in tranquil attitudes and peaceable feelings.

In spite of incompatibility between Greek and Hebrew understandings, we soon notice some Greek concepts and corresponding practices of peace entering the Christian church. Christian hermits who withdrew to a desert cave or the inner recesses of their own souls in search of spiritual harmony were esteemed. Thus concerns for the elemental aspects of social justice, where human relationships are ordered by God's covenant with His people, give way to concerns of a more spiritual nature. These concepts, which are really more Greek and pagan than Hebrew and Christian, have influenced the church throughout its history.

Peace among the Romans

Pax Romana was well known throughout the ancient world. Absence of armed rebellion was assured by the omnipresence of Roman military power. It was the kind of peace which required "keeping." The centurion in whose house Peter spoke those memorable words concerning God's word to Israel, "the gospel of peace by Jesus Christ" (Acts 10:36), was a peacemaker according to the definition which prevailed throughout the Roman Empire. He was an official in the army of occupation charged with keeping the peace, with maintaining law and order. Roman poets referred to the era of the Pax Romana as a Golden Age. Later Christians, including church historians, took up the same refrain. Among the peoples subjected to the evils of colonialism it was certainly no golden age. The Pax Romana was built upon the repression of all of the empire's enemies. From the time of Constantine in the fourth century, this understanding of peace, so contrary to the Spirit of Jesus and the meaning of shalom, has received the blessing of the church.

Another Roman contribution to the church's understanding of peace resulted from viewing the relationship between God and man in judicial terms. The Romans saw sin as transgression of divine law, and forgiveness in terms of penance, punishment, satisfaction, and absolution. This contributed to the development of the penitential or sacramental system in Roman Christianity which was designed to help the penitent sinner make peace with God.

Although Martin Luther, an Augustinian monk, reacted against the abuses of the Roman Catholic system, he was also a man of his times. He agonized within himself as he tried to find assurance of forgiveness. He continued to conceive of sin and forgiveness according to the Roman understanding. He found consolation in Paul's words, "Since we are justified by faith, we have peace with God through our Lord Jesus Christ" (Romans 5:1). Yet, under the influence of centuries of Roman thought, peace with God was still understood principally in terms of the inner assurance that one is the recipient of pardon granted by a merciful God. While this aspect is important, it scarcely begins to explore the rich dimensions of the biblical concept of shalom.

Although an understanding of shalom does not invalidate personal peace which gives inner assurance of being reconciled with God, it does underscore that biblical peace is much more. Peace is directly related to a new relationship with God within a covenanted community. Through God's grace a new community of peace and justice, based on love and sustained by the enabling presence of God's Spirit, becomes a possibility. Unfortunately, this communal social dimension of the gospel of peace continues to evade many Christians who conceive of peace with God in individual and inward terms. Due to these distortions of Roman origin, we fail to recognize the social and communitarian nature of the gospel of peace.

The new community of God's peace

Several examples from the New Testament will illustrate the potential of the gospel of peace for the creation of God's new community.

1. Ephesians 2:11-22 offers a glimpse of some of the marks of the new community which arise out of a response to the gospel of peace. To be "in Christ" (verse 13) is not so much an inner spiritual experience with the Spirit of Christ as concrete participation in a new humanity (verse 15) created by the grace of God manifested in Jesus Christ. The gospel of peace opens up a new relationship with God which becomes reality as we experience a new relationship of shalom with our fellow men.

In this community the differences and barriers which separated us from one another have been overcome: nationalism, regionalism, racism, prejudices based on difference of sex, the spirit of economic competition, cultural and religious and social differences which contribute to attitudes of superiority in some and inferiority in others. All are superseded in Christ. To be in Christ is to experience community, to share life at all levels of our existence, spiritual or material.

According to the New Testament, former enemies in this community of peace are reconciled and violence is eliminated in interpersonal relationships; persons of different races and nationalities participate in a brotherhood which is not merely spiritual or invisible, but which takes concrete social forms; the poor are succored and the broken are made whole. The function of the gospel of peace in Jesus Christ is restoration of that community of love and peace and justice which reflects God's

intention for life among His people. It is the life of the
kingdom that Jesus inaugurated which has become a
human possibility through the Holy Spirit.

2. The form which the primitive community in
Jerusalem took provides another dimension of the gospel
of peace. Where the gospel of peace is heard and obeyed,
the Holy Spirit creates a new community characterized by
deep mutual concern and openness. In describing this
community Luke wrote, "The company of those who
believed were of one heart and soul, and no one said that
any of the things which he possessed was *his own,* but they
had everything in *common"* (Acts 4:32). Perhaps the
quality of life experienced in this community can be best
understood by comparing the two conflicting principles
of social relationships mentioned.

Self-centeredness. One principle is the spirit of self-
centeredness expressed by the words "his own." This
orientation concentrates on one's self, one's own, on
ownership, and on that which is owned. This self-centered
stance is idolatrous and isolating. It excludes others from
fellowship. Individualism and private use of goods are the
results. This spirit was rejected by the Christian community in Jerusalem.

Although the primitive church recognized the spirit of
self-centeredness for what it was, this cannot be said for
much of the church throughout history. Modern Western
societies are generally based on private ownership with a
social contract regulating competition and other forms of
self-interest within acceptable limits by a kind of balance
of power. We can expect secular societies to organize according to this principle. But it is tragic that the church,

too, has often organized its life around these democratic principles which depend on a balance of power. This is a form of Roman pax rather than the shalom which Jesus and the apostles envisioned.

Sharing. The other spirit, the one characterizing the church in Jerusalem, is that which shares a common life. This is the spirit of community in which all participate for the common good. Koinonia is not the negation of the individual person. In this community of peace the individual finds fullest realization. In this community one is delivered from the temptation of idolatry because God is at the center of human relationships and life is shared by the power of the Spirit.

Under the impulse of the Holy Spirit the congregation continued the practices of the Year of Jubilee, or year of remission, that Jesus had announced at the beginning of His ministry and had carried out in the circle of disciples. "The Spirit of the Lord is upon me . . . he has anointed me . . . to proclaim the acceptable year of the Lord" (Luke 4:18). According to the Jubilee the earth and its fullness are the Lord's; therefore, its resources are to be shared to meet the needs of His people. To correct accumulated inequities a periodic year of remission was proclaimed in which debts were pardoned, slaves were freed, and family inheritance which had been lost through adverse economic circumstances was restored.

In an attempt to practice concretely the gospel of peace which Jesus proclaimed, the church in Jerusalem was led by the Spirit to renew the year of remission. It may not be necessary to organize the church of the twentieth century on the exact pattern of the primitive community in

Jerusalem in order to renew it. But if renewal is to happen, it will be necessary to take seriously the Spirit and fundamentally communitarian forms of life which arise out of the shalom of God which Jesus proclaimed.

3. Finally, it should be remembered that as Christians are peacemakers, they are God's sons (Matthew 5:9). We become like our Father as we practice and proclaim the gospel of peace. As peacemakers in our world we are called to solidarity with the poor and the oppressed, to contribute to the healing of the sick and afflicted, to feed the hungry, to care for the rejected and the lonely, to proclaim the message of freedom and peace to the enslaved, to invite all men to be reconciled to God—that is, to act as God has acted in the world in Jesus of Nazareth.

The person reached by the gospel of peace and made new by the power of God's Spirit will not be able to tolerate with a clear conscience self-centeredness in any of its obvious or more subtle forms: a competitive spirit, undue desire for recognition, accumulation of goods, urge to dominate, tendency to discriminate. The Christian who dares to live the gospel of peace will be at odds with society. The peacemaker cannot allow himself to be pressed into the world's mold.

In the ancient world the term peacemaker designated two very different kinds of people: the Roman emperor and the followers of Jesus. The meaning of the designation in the first case was determined by the criteria of efficacy. To be a peacemaker was to do what was necessary to promote the welfare of the empire. The substance of the designation in the case of Christians was determined by Jesus. Jesus the peacemaker furnishes both the substance and the method of our peacemaking. His way of peace determines the form which our presence and proclamation take in the world.

To be a peacemaker is to participate in God's community of peace, renewed by the power of His Spirit as we already anticipate life in His kingdom. Shalom.

6. THE CHURCH:
A MISSIONARY COMMUNITY

Witness of the early church

An extraordinary quality of life characterized the
Christian community described in the Acts of the
Apostles. The beauty of their communal practices, intensity and fervor of worship, courageous witness under
pressures of persecution, gospel lifestyle—all of these
marks appear attractive.

Sometimes we are tempted to idealize this little block of
the church's history. But the primitive church also had its
problems. In a congregation where "there was not a needy
person among them," some were moved to protest what
they felt was unequal distribution of goods within the
community. Questions of religious ceremonies and
matters pertaining to missionary workers were debated
bitterly. Even with the advent of pentecostal power, the
weaknesses of the Twelve were not overcome fully.

However, these defects dare not blind us to the
seriousness with which the early Christians took their life
as the new community of the Messiah. Acts describes a
community radically conformed to the Spirit and lifestyle
of its Lord, which in turn led to a socially nonconformist
attitude toward the world. Values which determined
lifestyle and direction were clearly visible.

This kind of community exudes clear missionary
possibilities. In a generally conformed society, a morally

nonconformist community will be highly visible. A community which, contrary to everyone else, shares its goods, loves its enemies as well as its friends, keeps its word, will naturally communicate something of the reconciling love of God to the world beyond. So the very forms of the church's obedience constituted a powerful missionary witness. This is the missionary visibility of which Jesus spoke, "You are the light of the world. A city set on a hill cannot be hid" (Matthew 5:14).

Verbal testimony to what God had done, and was continuing to do, for the salvation of His people, was another missionary element in the life of the primitive church. Beginning with the experience of the pentecostal community Peter proclaimed that God had shown Jesus to be both Lord and Messiah by the resurrection (Acts 2:32-36). Undisputable evidence of this was the pouring out of the Holy Spirit (Acts 2:33).

The message of Peter—which, we shall note later, contained precisely the same elements as the message of Jesus Himself—was: Repent, become a part of God's new people gathered around Jesus the Messiah and you will receive the gift of the Holy Spirit, bestowed by God upon all His children in the new messianic era enabling them to live the life of the kingdom of God (Acts 2:38, 39). His warning to save themselves from a crooked generation equals an invitation to find their salvation in the new people of God gathered around His Messiah (Acts 2:40, 41). This is the meaning of Luke's statement that "the Lord added to their number day by day those who were being saved" (Acts 2:47).

The fundamental witness of the apostles was to Christ accompanied by an invitation to change in spirit and attitude, in lifestyle and relationships. In short, it was a call to repent in order to participate in God's new community.

What is the gospel?

The terms "gospel" and "evangelize" are used with great frequency in the church, but their essential meanings have not always been fully understood. Gospel often refers to the invitation to accept the forgiveness of sins, and to the process of making this invitation known.

Originally gospel was neither a religious nor an individual term, but secular and collective. It meant simply good news. But it was not just any kind of news. In ancient Greece, where the term was used before it was employed by the New Testament writers, gospel was used to indicate important information on which the welfare of a state might depend. This might include news of victory in a decisive battle which assured the freedom of the people, or notice of the birth of a male heir in the royal family assuring continuation of the dynasty. This is precisely the sense in which gospel is used in the New Testament. It is the good news that the kingdom of God is about to be established among people.

This kingdom is so unique that nothing short of full repentance will prepare men and women to participate in it. Repentance implies a conversion, or turnaround, of the spirit or mind. Sometimes it is described as a radical change of attitude. But New Testament repentance which prepares men and women to live under the reign of God moves beyond change of attitude to concrete social practices. John the Baptist warned that repentance included an act of the will together with its corresponding fruits. For common people repentance implied sharing goods with those in need. For tax collectors repentance meant becoming honest men. For soldiers repentance meant treating the people with consideration and being less violent (Luke 3:10-14).

This was the message of both John the Baptist and Jesus: "Repent, for the kingdom of heaven is at hand" (Matthew 3:2; 4:17). Immediately Matthew informs us that this message about the kingdom of heaven is gospel (Matthew 4:23). But how was this kingdom to be realized? It was essentially with this question that Jesus struggled in the wilderness temptations.

First, Jesus was tempted to be an economic messiah. He refused that option because He understood that the real needs of humankind are much more inclusive (Matthew 4: 3, 4; compare John 6:15). Jesus was also tempted to establish Himself as messiah by a political-religious coup through exercising miraculous powers. He refused that alternative as being out of harmony with the nature of God (Matthew 4:5, 7; compare Matthew 21: 12-17; John 2:17). Jesus was tempted, finally, to base His messiahship on instruments of political power. He refused this route because it involved making satanic concessions instead of trusting in His heavenly Father (Matthew 4: 8-10; compare Matthew 26:52, 53). These temptations were all aspects of the nationalistic vision, and until the last moment His followers were asking Jesus if He was going to restore Israel's political independence (Acts 1:6).

Another kind of strategy

But the strategy of Jesus was of another kind. Rather than allowing Himself to be pressed into a messianic

mold, He understood the will of His Father to be
otherwise. At His baptism two important things hap-
pened. First, the Holy Spirit came upon Him as a prelude
to the new creation (compare Genesis 1:2), anointing Him
for messianic mission (Acts 10:36-38). Second, the words
which are heard from heaven designated Jesus as the true
servant Messiah announced by Isaiah (42:1).

In light of this event we are able to understand the next
steps of Jesus as Matthew recorded them. Jesus began to
visit the villages of Galilee "teaching in their synagogues
and preaching the gospel of the kingdom and healing
every disease and every infirmity among the people"
(Matthew 4:23). This was messianic activity, not according to the nationalistic political expectations of most of
the Jewish people, but in the tradition of the vision of the
suffering servant (Isaiah 42: 1-9; 49:1-6; 50:4-11; 52:13—
53:12). In this context Jesus' healing ministry is best understood (Matthew 8:7; Acts 10:38).

Another thing Jesus began to do following His bap-
tismal commission was to invite men to voluntarily leave
their occupations and follow Him. Their number even-
tually reached twelve, representative of the tribes of Israel
in the new messianic community in formation.

Matthew places the Sermon on the Mount in this context. It is a résumé in which Jesus set forth the new spirit
and lifestyle characteristic of the new community. It was
an inaugural address stating the program and policies of
the new messianic regime.

• He begins by describing the citizens of the new
kingdom and the underlying spirit which inspires their
new life (5:3-16).

• He deals with interpersonal relationships in the

kingdom. Problems mentioned include anger, illicit sex-
ual relations, untruthfulness, vengeance and hate toward
the enemy (5:17-48).

 • He treats the relationship between kingdom citizens
and their king. This includes warnings about the spirit
behind religious practices (6:1-6, 16-18), a prayer model
(6:7-15), and a description of the attitude of kingdom
citizens toward possessions (6:19-34).

 • Finally He counsels concerning interpersonal
relationships in the kingdom (7:1-12) and warns about the
seriousness with which kingdom concerns should be
taken and the dangers which kingdom citizens will face
(7:13-27).

Messianic program demands are overwhelming. Impossible from a human perspective, they become possible
because the Lord—anointed "with the Holy Spirit and
with power" (Acts 10:38; compare Matthew 4:16)—is "he
who baptizes with the Holy Spirit" (John 1:33), thereby
enabling men and women to live the kingdom way. According to Luke, it was precisely within the context of
Jesus' Sermon on the Mount that He promises, "The
heavenly Father [will] give the Holy Spirit to those who
ask him!" (Luke 11:13). To live the life of the kingdom
means counting on the Spirit of the King. To live the life
of Christ is impossible without the Spirit of Christ.

All this is gospel

Back to our question: What is the gospel? According
to Jesus, the One who came announcing the gospel of the
kingdom, ALL THIS IS GOSPEL: The announcement
that the kingdom is coming; the invitation to change
radically and join the new people of God who live under

the lordship of Jesus Christ, the spirit and the substance of this new life in community, and finally, the power of the Spirit of Christ Himself which enables one to live the new life.

In considering the gospel of the kingdom we have studied the first part of Matthew, but this emphasis also occurs at other places in the New Testament. While not generally noticed, Acts begins and ends with the kingdom theme. Luke reports that this was the theme of conversation between Jesus and His disciples during the forty days after the resurrection (1:3). When Paul finally reached Rome he spent two years "preaching the kingdom of God and teaching about the Lord Jesus Christ quite openly and unhindered" (28-31).

Someone has said that Jesus came preaching the kingdom, but the apostles simply preached Christ. This is only part truth, because to preach Jesus is to proclaim the kingdom, for He is Lord. Even though the theme of apostolic preaching was Christ, in reality that meant proclaiming the gospel of the kingdom.

The Twelve were sent out with the same message that Jesus proclaimed: "And preach as you go, saying, 'The kingdom of heaven is at hand' " (Matthew 10:7). They were also charged to heal the sick, cleanse the lepers, cast out demons. Their mission, just as their Lord's, was modeled after the pattern of the suffering servant. Luke identifies this missionary activity as gospel—"preaching the gospel and healing everywhere" (Luke 9:6).

The mission of the seventy follows the same pattern— lifestyle consistent with the values of the new messianic community (nonresistance and abandonment to the providence of God instead of trusting in their possessions), healing in the tradition of the servant of Yahweh, announcement that the kingdom of God is approaching (Luke 10:1-12).

The church has generally assumed that the central gospel message is the good news of personal well-being free for the taking and with minimal demands. We hear of receiving Jesus, forgiveness, love, happiness, peace of soul. The difficult part is expected to come later under a different name. It is called Christian growth, sanctification, or the second blessing, but this is another step. Although one has been saved by the grace of God, he will still be a sinner, it is sometimes said. Such theological maneuvers have been used to assure the salvation of those who have not found it feasible to live according to Jesus' Spirit, words, and deeds.

But as we have already noted, according to Jesus, the gospel includes all these things. This leads us to another question: What does it mean to evangelize?

What does it mean to evangelize?

The Great Commission (Matthew 28:18-20) has been used extensively to justify and encourage the missionary enterprise. But rarely has this text been understood in the radical sense of its original context. The church, rather, has tended to read it (and the rest of the Bible for that matter) through the filter of distortions accumulated in the slow process of social domestication. The following elements are offered as aids to a more adequate understanding of the commission.

1. *Jesus has already received the kingdom.* "All authority in heaven and on earth has been given to me." (Versions which have "*is* given" do not translate faithfully

the past tense of the Greek verb.) Jesus of Nazareth, the suffering servant commissioned by God, who died rather than compromise the integrity of His cause by depending on Peter's sword or the protection of twelve legions of angels, came preaching the kingdom. He is now Lord of the universe, Lord of a kingdom whose dimensions are both temporal and cosmic. Concerning the final victory of His cause, there can be no doubt. The real significance of human history flows through this kingdom. All else is destined to perish unless it submits to the spirit and the lifestyle characteristic of this kingdom. From this perspective we see the absolute importance of the gospel as Jesus has defined it.

2. *Jesus ordered His followers to proceed as He had.* "Go therefore and make disciples of all nations, baptizing them in the name of the Father and of the Son and of the Holy Spirit, teaching them to observe all that I have commanded you." This commission converted the disciples (followers) of Jesus into apostles (those who are sent). The rest of the New Testament is the story of the vicissitudes of these missioners, going throughout the Roman Empire and beyond, sometimes as prisoners of Roman justice, sometimes as itinerant artisans or merchants, sometimes simply as Christians fleeing from their persecutors. This mobility, in itself, was an act of radical protest against the spirit which prizes material security, social acceptance, and comfortable living, because it implied willingness to sacrifice even life itself to incarnate and proclaim the gospel.

To make disciples of Jesus is really the fundamental element in this commission. To evangelize is to make disciples of Jesus. The apostles knew from their own ex-

perience what this implied. It meant following Jesus in absolute obedience and personal abandonment. It implied
changing occupations and sharing possessions. It included subordinating personal family interests to the demands
of new loyalties. It brought with it a whole series of dif-
ficulties and social persecution. It meant being willing to
risk one's own life and security.

The Great Commission laid upon Jesus' followers the
task of making disciples in a way which bears little
resemblance to the results which have often characterized
modern evangelism. To invite persons to salvation as if
this could be experienced apart from discipleship was
simply outside the realm of imagination for Jesus and the
apostles. The case of the rich young ruler, narrated in
every one of the synoptics, clearly shows the impossibility
of enjoying eternal life independently of the most fundamental demands of discipleship. To become a disciple
includes voluntary and absolute submission to Jesus
Christ, symbolized in baptism and concrete adherence to
the kind of lifestyle which Jesus described in the Sermon
on the Mount. We are not permitted to define discipleship
according to our own convenience or our own moral
possibilities.

3. *Jesus promises to accompany His disciples in the
risky adventures of kingdom life until the end.* "I am with
you always, to the close of the age." A discipleship which,
humanly speaking, is impossible, is transformed into a
joyful possibility because Jesus Christ who is already
Sovereign of the universe is He who has promised to be
with us and to dwell within us. It is the presence of Jesus in
His disciple community which makes the gospel we
proclaim eternally contemporary.

What are the implications?

We have noted the missionary stance of the apostolic church characterized by the quality of its life, as well as its verbal testimony to that which was happening in its midst. We have described the meaning which Jesus gave through His life and teachings to the term gospel. We have noted some of the radical dimensions of the Great Commission which have often escaped Christians. What, then, are the implications for our understanding of the church's missionary task?

1. *The church needs to experience again a contemporary gospel.* When the church is the community in which Jesus is Lord—where the life of the kingdom is already being lived, where the works of servanthood lead to wholeness (salvation) among needy persons, where every separating barrier is destroyed and community is created—then it will become clear that Jesus Christ reigns and that His Spirit lives and works among His people. Verbal evangelistic witness in this kind of setting will identify and interpret the current mighty acts of God.

2. *The central task of evangelism is forming disciple communities.* Evangelism is not simply saving individuals from hell for heaven, nor inviting them to repentance and then leaving them to struggle alone to be faithful to their confession that Jesus is Lord. Evangelism is calling men and women to repentance and inviting them to become a part of the community of God's people which participate even now and here on earth in the kingdom of God which will finally come in all of its fullness.

3. *The radical New Testament concept of discipleship must be rediscovered.* This means that the words of the Lord carry absolute authority for the disciple. In no cir-

cumstances is the disciple in a position to negotiate with his Lord the conditions of his discipleship. He has been freed from the tyranny of sin to become a slave of Christ (Matthew 6:24). Furthermore, this implies conformity to the attitudes and Spirit of Jesus. Not only His words, but the Spirit and intentions of the Lord are authoritative. The disciple has no choice but to assume the mind of Christ who renounced recourse to coercive power and assumed the condition of a servant (Philippians 2:5-11).

Discipleship implies conformity to the concrete deportment of Jesus. To act as Jesus acted will provide concrete ethical substance to the lifestyle of the disciple. As in the case of Jesus, this will cause the disciple to live against the dominant moral current. This has consequences for the way the disciple of Jesus gets and uses money, attitudes toward the exercise of power, relationships in marriage, and other interpersonal spheres. Only that community which knows in experience the meaning of discipleship will be capable of making disciples. To show political awareness, to be socially concerned, to be evangelistic, to organize for extension, to experience church growth— these are relatively easy. But to form disciples of Jesus goes beyond all of these and is possible only in a community which practices discipleship.

4. *The community of Jesus Christ is the kingdom in which all of human history will ultimately find its meaning.* To be so convinced is of tremendous consequence. Negatively, it means that the value system which predominates secular history is inverted. The world's centers of power and instruments of influence are not of ultimate consequence. The church must, therefore, resist the temptation to use missionary methods simply because

they appear to be effective. The measure of the church's missionary methods, as well as its end, must be Jesus.

Menno Simons described the testimony of the church in these terms: "that the name, will, Word, and ordinance of Christ are confidently confessed in the face of all cruelty, tyranny, tumult, fire, sword and violence of the world and sustained unto the end" *(Complete Works,* page 741). Menno was concerned that Christian testimony be given even in the face of opposition without making moral concessions. The response of the hearers to the church's message was not for the moment the principal element. What was fundamental for Menno was that the witness resist the temptation to dilute or distort his testimony according to the likes of the hearers.

An adequate vision of the dimensions of Christ's kingdom will free us from the temptation to sacrifice the substance of the gospel message for evangelistic "effectiveness." Even though it may be costly, the true criterion for evaluating our evangelistic practices is the formation of disciple communities obedient to Jesus.

The gospel is the good news of Jesus Christ inviting persons to enter into a new life of love and obedience in the context of the community of the kingdom which anticipates the ultimate reign of God over the cosmos. Hallelujah!

John Driver grew up in Hesston, Kansas, where he graduated from Hesston Academy. He received his BA from Goshen College, Goshen, Indiana, in 1950, his BD from Goshen Biblical Seminary in 1960, and his STM from Perkins School of Theology, Dallas, Texas, in 1967. He married Bonita Landis. They are the parents of Cynthia, Wilfred, and Jonathan.

The Drivers have been working as part of the Mennonite Board of Missions (Elkhart, Indiana) Latin team since 1951. Earlier, John served with Mennonite Central Committee and Mennonite Relief Committee in Puerto Rico from 1945-48 and Bonita from 1947-48. They then served as missionaries in Puerto Rico from 1951-66 and in Uruguay from 1967-74.

As part of his missionary assignment in Uruguay,

John Driver was professor of church history and New Testament at Seminario Evangelico Menonita de Teologia, Montevideo. He also served the seminary until its closing in late 1974 as dean of studies from 1967, and as acting rector from 1972. The Drivers spent ten months in Spain in 1975 preparatory to a continuing Mennonite witness in that country.

John is the author of *Comunidad y Compromiso,* published in Buenos Aires, Argentina, in 1974, as well as a number of published articles. He contributed the lead chapter in *Being God's Missionary Community,* a symposium of reflections on Mennonite missions 1945-75. He is co-author with Samuel Escobar of *Christian Mission and Social Justice* to be published in 1977 by Herald Press in association with the Institute of Mennonite Studies, as part of the Missionary Studies series.